Original title:
Woven in Wildflowers

Copyright © 2025 Creative Arts Management OÜ
All rights reserved.

Author: Colin Harrington
ISBN HARDBACK: 978-1-80567-005-6
ISBN PAPERBACK: 978-1-80567-085-8

Harmony in Nature's Flourish

In the meadow where daisies dance,
Bees wear tiny pants by chance.
Butterflies laugh, flit, and swoop,
While ants form a marching troupe.

Squirrels debate on acorn clout,
While rabbits hop with a joyous shout.
A frog on a lily pad sings a tune,
Echoing laughter beneath the moon.

Sunflowers grin at the passing breeze,
Tickling the toes of old oak trees.
Ladybugs roll with glee on a leaf,
Spreading delight beyond belief.

Nature's chaos, a whimsical play,
Where critters frolic throughout the day.
With every chuckle, each giggly sound,
Life blooms merrily all around.

Blossoms Beneath the Sky

Daisies dancing in a breeze,
They wiggle like they've got no knees.
Bumblebees with tiny grins,
Buzzing round like they're all kin.

Buttercups, a golden sea,
Playing hide and seek with me.
Tulips twirl in a floral show,
Making petals flutter to and fro.

Fabric of Flora and Sunlight

Sunflowers stretching up so tall,
Heads so big, they'll surely fall.
Petals bright as a painter's hue,
Chasing rays like it's a view.

Cacti wear their prickly hats,
Complaining 'bout the lazy bats.
Dandelions' seeds fly in swirls,
Each one dreams of spinster girls.

Nature's Vibrant Patchwork

Poppies blushing in the sun,
Telling stories, oh what fun!
Lavender scents float through the air,
While ants march on, without a care.

Marigolds with golden crowns,
Chasing away those sleepy frowns.
Butterflies flit, a colorful sight,
Deciding which flower feels just right.

Harmony in Petal and Leaf

Petunias gossiping in a row,
Whispering things we'll never know.
Ferns creating a leafy dance,
Growing tall, they take their chance.

In a garden where laughter grows,
Every bloom has its own prose.
Roses smirk as they take a stand,
While daisies plot a flower band.

A Tapestry of Shimmering Colors

Amidst the blooms, bees take a dive,
In search of nectar, they jive and thrive.
A daisy advises, "Be bold, take flight!"
While tulips gossip, gossip day and night.

Butterflies dance in a colorful spree,
A sight so silly, it cracks me, you see!
They flap and stumble, what a funny sight,
In this vibrant quilt, all takes delight.

Echoes of Meadow Melodies

In fields of laughter, voices do sing,
A chorus of crickets, what joy they bring!
A squirrel's quick chatter, a cheeky little tease,
Makes even the flowers shake with the breeze.

Dandelions wish for their chance to fly,
"Just one puff, please!" they beg as they sigh.
A slight breeze chuckles, they scatter like rice,
A riot of fluff—ah, nature's own spice!

Vibrancy in Vines and Blooms

The vines twist and tangle, a silly parade,
With fantasies of becoming a grand charade.
Petunias giggle, their colors so bright,
As the sun's warm rays cause antics of light.

A bumblebee's buzz is a comical tune,
He fumbles and tumbles while swooping too soon.
"Not on my petals!" the roses declare,
As petals flail wildly, but no one can care!

The Poetry of a Blooming Day

Morning arrives with a hop and a skip,
The daisies chuckle, throwing nature a quip.
A sunbeam outshines all the serious stuff,
As laughter and pollen blend into a fluff.

The day rolls on with a joyful spree,
A ladybug winks; it's a sight to see!
With colors so bright, and laughter so free,
This garden's antics, a comedy spree!

Garden Symphony and Sundrenched Sounds

In a garden where the daisies dance,
Bees are buzzing, stealing glances.
A carrot wears a little hat,
While onions sing and tap their spat.

The tomatoes giggle, red and round,
While potatoes play beneath the ground.
Squirrels serenade the sunlit beams,
As the wind whispers our leafy dreams.

Embracing the Wild and Free

In meadows bright, the rabbits prance,
Their floppy ears in a sunshine trance.
A ladybug in shades so bold,
Doodles a story waiting to be told.

The chickens dress in fancy threads,
While grasshoppers hop on leafy beds.
A butterfly politely swoops,
While ducks imitate popular loops.

Brushstrokes of Wild Beauty

A paintbrush swirls beneath the pines,
With colors splashed on vines and twines.
Sunflowers grin in golden rows,
Tickling bees with secret prose.

The air is sweet with laughter's breeze,
As flower crowns meet bumblebee tease.
Each petal's essence takes a chance,
In nature's unpredictable dance.

Living Colors of an Untamed Land

In vibrant fields where laughter sings,
The daisies dance on fluttering wings.
A poppy whispers a silly joke,
While hedgehogs take turns in a cloak.

Buttercups hold a frolicsome feast,
As butterflies flit, to say the least.
Frogs compete in a croak-off show,
In colors bright, they put on a glow.

Verses of Sun and Shadow

Beneath a sun that likes to tease,
The daisies dance in fervent breeze.
A honeybee buzzes with a grin,
"Why worry? Just join the spin!"

A carpet stitched in shades of cheer,
With blooms that giggle, drawing near.
The butterflies flutter, not shy at all,
"Join us for the flower ball!"

Nature's Chorus in Full Bloom

In fields where colorful chaos reigns,
The flowers gossip, sharing gains.
"Did you hear of that vine's tall tale?"
"Oh yes! She tripped, it was so pale!"

The daisies shout with gleeful might,
"We're the stars of this floral night!"
While poppies sway, they chant in play,
"Catch the breeze, come frolic, yay!"

Ode to the Blossoms' Whisper

Oh petals soft, with colors bright,
You tickle noses with sheer delight.
"Time for tea!" the roses chant,
"But bring the sugar, we're sure to slant!"

The tulips nod, with hats tipped low,
In secret chats, they steal the show.
"You heard about that clumsy bee?"
"He flew too close, flew straight at me!"

Threads of Growth Beneath the Sky

In the hush of morn, when dew is fresh,
The flowers giggle, oh what a mess!
"Did you see how that one just fell?"
"Let's not tell, we'll keep it swell!"

The grass joins in, with curls of green,
"Watch out! A squirrel! What's that unseen?"
They point and laugh, the scene so fine,
"Nature's antics, a grand design!"

Flourish in the Fields of Joy

In fields of laughter, we run and play,
With daisies and jokes, we brighten the day.
The bees do a dance, a buzzing parade,
While we trip on roots, all plans are delayed.

Buttercups giggle, they tickle our feet,
As we tumble and roll in this floral retreat.
With each silly stumble, we harvest some glee,
Nature's our playground, wild and carefree.

Ties of the Earth and Sky

The sun and the soil have giggly ties,
As clouds tell the flowers their comical lies.
Roses wear sunglasses, trying to show,
That they know the secrets of how to glow.

Dandelion puffs make a fuss on the breeze,
Like toddlers with dreams, they're sure to appease.
They scatter their jokes, a whimsical flight,
Leaving chuckles and smiles beneath the sun's light.

Nature's Languages of Color

The hues have a chuckle, a riotous cheer,
When violet socks mingle with yellow gear.
Crayons in petals, a colorful spree,
As the trees start to giggle, come dance with me!

Orange and pink, they throw a paint fight,
While green grass says: 'You shall not take flight!'
With a tickle of sunshine, they sparkle and shine,
Nature's a court jest, and we are divine.

Petals in the Wake of Wonder

With petals that whisper, 'Come join the fun,'
We chase after breezes beneath the bright sun.
The tulips are jesters, with jokes up their sleeves,
As butterflies giggle, hiding behind leaves.

A snapdragon smiles, with a wink and a nod,
While lily pads chat, thinking they're so odd.
In nature's grand circus, we leap and we twirl,
Among whimsical blooms, our laughter unfurl.

A Dance of Petals and Dreams

In a field where daisies twirl,
The butterflies begin to swirl.
A dandelion sneezes with glee,
And tickles the bumblebee.

A ladybug lost her way,
Chasing ants who love to play.
While grasshoppers sing their tune,
Underneath the laughing moon.

Tulips giggle, roses grin,
As the sun begins to spin.
A bumblebee bought a hat,
Who knew they'd look like that?

With every step, a flower shouts,
Dancing on without a doubt.
In this bloom of jolly cheer,
We'll stay here, what could be clearer?

Journey through the Colorful Veil

Through the garden, colors fly,
Petunias wink as bees go by.
The lilies laugh, oh what a sight,
As violets tease in playful flight.

A snail dons shades, looking cool,
While frogs conduct a jumping school.
A sunflower, tall and bold,
Wants to trade its seeds for gold.

An evening breeze brings jokes anew,
As poppies dance, they wave to you.
With every step, we trip and fall,
On hidden blooms that call us all.

Through the hues, so vibrant and bright,
Nature's humor takes its flight.
Giggling petals, prancing leaves,
In this journey, joy achieves.

Threads of Nature's Tapestry

In a meadow, colors gleam,
With butterflies, we chase a dream.
The grass is sly, it pulls our socks,
As we wander past the rocks.

A thistle whispers, 'Watch your feet!'
While daisies drop their lunch to eat.
The ants march in a funny line,
Claiming breadcrumbs as their mine.

A wandering bee, so full of cheer,
Sings a tune only we can hear.
Roses chuckle, basking in sun,
Each petal says, 'Let's have some fun!'

Threads of laughter stitch the breeze,
Amidst the blooms, we twist with ease.
In this wacky floral space,
Nature serves its best embrace.

Blossoms Beneath the Sky

Beneath the sky, in bursts of hues,
The flowers break out in silly snooze.
Daffodils play peek-a-boo,
While violets dance in morning dew.

A bumblebee hums a buzzing tune,
Claiming each nectar as a boon.
Pansies gossip, sharing the news,
About a cat that sings the blues.

Morning glories stretch and yawn,
As butterflies weave into the dawn.
A rainbow makes the blossoms sigh,
'Oh joy, oh joy, we can fly high!'

With petals swaying to and fro,
In this garden, we steal the show.
Blooming laughter fills the air,
With each bouquet, we dance with flair.

The Tranquil Brush of Spring

A bee with a beret buzzes near,
Painting petals with sticky cheer.
The daisies gossip, the tulips tease,
While ants parade, declaring peace.

The sun yawns wide, a lazy glow,
Tickling blooms, making them grow.
A dandelion dons a crown so bright,
Announcing royalty with all its might.

The clouds play tag, a fluffy crew,
While flowers giggle in morning dew.
Nature's jesters, sprightly and spry,
Tickle the sky as they wave goodbye.

With butterflies chatting, it's quite a sight,
In this jolly realm, laughter takes flight.
Each petal's a punchline, soft and light,
Spring's joyful brush dances out of sight.

Splashes of Life Amongst the Green

A frog takes a leap, what a silly show,
Landing on a lily, it's quite the throw.
Grasshoppers giggle with every jump,
Discussing the antics of this little lump.

Sunshine giggles, a warm, bright friend,
Tickling the flowers without an end.
The squirrels convene for a nutty debate,
While birds chirp secrets they've learned from fate.

A snail with swagger, gliding with grace,
Takes the slow lane, always in place.
"Why rush?" it muses with a gleeful grin,
"When the best things in life are found from within?"

The butterflies twirl in a whimsical dance,
Drawing the gaze of a curious lance.
Each splash of color, a chuckle, a cheer,
Life's playful brush brings smiles near and dear.

Celestial Blooms and Grounded Dreams

Stars on the ground, or so they claim,
With daffodils practicing their fame.
A cosmos of petals, swaying with flair,
Dreaming of space while grounded out there.

A bumblebee bursts into a song,
With notes so sweet, but not for long.
Cosmic giggles from twinkling skies,
As flowers laugh at their own surprise.

"Mars is red, but I'm the queen!"
A rose proclaims in a leafy scene.
The tulips respond with a colorful shout,
"Who needs the stars when we've got clout?"

As moonlight tumbles on beds of green,
Dancing with dreams in a floral scene.
Each bloom a tale, each petal a jest,
Grounded in laughter, forever blessed.

Secrets in the Soil

Under the surface, a chuckle creeps,
As worms tell stories, the soil keeps.
A gopher giggles, digging around,
Unearthing secrets, oh what a sound!

Roots whisper tales of yesterday's fun,
About sunlit days and how they run.
"Let's loosen the dirt, do a little dance,
And make the sprout's day by giving a chance!"

A hidden toad hops with a grin,
Sharing jokes with a shy little pin.
"Why did the seed bring a blanket to bed?
To not catch a cold when it sprouted its head!"

In the dark, laughter turns into light,
As nature's jesters delight in the night.
Secrets held tight, in soil's warm embrace,
A funny world hidden, a magical place.

Celestial Dances of Floral Flames

A daisy in a tutu spins,
While bumblebees play violin.
The sunflowers sway like they're on stage,
Throwing petals, what a rage!

Dandelions puff like clouds of dreams,
As ladybugs plot in sunbeam schemes.
Grasshoppers dance with wild delight,
While frogs croak jokes, 'Oh what a sight!'

Butterflies twirl in wacky pairs,
Wings painted in the laughter of airs.
Each bloom joins in the zany show,
Nature's circus, oh what a glow!

Bees are buzzing their witty lines,
Every petal puts on rhymes.
In this garden, nonsense reigns,
Where silly laughter never wanes!

The Heartbeat of the Meadow

In the field where the goats play chess,
I found a flower that wore a dress.
It giggled at the buzzing flies,
And winked at me with silly eyes.

The grass tickles toes of crickets loud,
While daisies tease the passing cloud.
A butterfly plays hide and seek,
Its colorful antics make me squeak!

Nearby, a snail runs a slow race,
While ants march on with laser grace.
The wind whispers jokes to the trees,
As flowers bob like they're pleased.

This meadow's heartbeat is full of cheer,
Each bloom sings songs that I can hear.
And as I laugh beneath the sun,
Nature's fun has just begun!

Immerse in Nature's Quilt

Underneath a patchwork sky,
A patch of grass starts to comply.
The flowers giggle, tangle tight,
Making fun of the birds in flight.

The daisies gather for tea and chats,
While squirrels dance wearing silly hats.
A rosemary sprout starts a debate,
With thyme over how to marinate.

Each leaf whispers gossip, don't you know?
While poppies laugh at the daffodil's glow.
Nature knits with threads of fun,
In this quilt, we all are one.

As the night falls, the moon takes a peek,
At the blossoms that laugh and speak.
In this garden, joy unfolds,
Every secret happiness told!

Textures of the Untamed

In a jungle where the wild things grow,
A cucumber dreams of becoming a show.
The plants wear fluff, without a care,
And roots twist like they're doing hair.

Fungi flicker with fairy lights,
While hedgehogs argue over jumping heights.
The sun beams in with a cheeky grin,
As critters find mischief to begin.

Thorns bear witness, the rose is bold,
While the violets gossip about gold.
Tangled in laughter, brambles chime,
Creating a rhythm, a silly rhyme.

Earthworms play hopscotch, quite a sight,
Getting muddy with pure delight.
In this untamed, joyous space,
Nature's textures bring a funny face!

Meadow Whispers and Sunlit Dreams

In fields where daisies tell a tale,
The butterflies giggle, they never fail.
A bumblebee wearing its tiny hat,
Buzzing 'bout gossip like a chitchat.

The sun spills laughter over each flower,
Tickling petals in a sunlit shower.
Grasshoppers play hopscotch, oh what fun!
While daisies dance under the cheeky sun.

A squirrel recites a wildflower's rhyme,
As ants march in sync, keeping the time.
Nature's jesters, in vibrant attire,
Making the meadow a stage of desire.

So let us frolic in this patch of mirth,
Where whimsy and wonder weave through the earth.
For laughter blooms in every sweet scent,
In this cheerful wild, where joy is spent.

Petals of a Forgotten Spring

In a corner where the old blooms sigh,
Petals gossip 'neath the bluebird's eye.
They joke of hoarding the last spring dew,
While the dandelion bids all adieu.

A calendar lies with pages blown,
Forgotten parties by the bees overgrown.
Tulips swaying with their heads held high,
Embarrassed by daffodils passing by.

Blossoms tell stories of awkward dates,
Of bees that fumble, and shy little mates.
Each petal chuckles in the warm sun's beam,
Sharing secrets of spring's grand dream.

Though time may chase with a zephyr's tease,
These petals remain, flapping like the breeze.
In whispers and giggles, they'll forever cling,
To the laughter and joy that each spring will bring.

The Dance of Colorful Petals

In a twirling whirl of colors so bright,
Petals are dancing, what a fabulous sight!
Sunflowers leap with their heads held high,
While poppies sway, feeling quite spry.

A rose winks, posing like it's on stage,
"Watch me show off!" it shouts with a rage.
Daffodils laugh, they can't find the beat,
Tripping on roots with their clumsy little feet.

In this garden soirée, all critters partake,
The ants do the cha-cha, while frogs take a break.
Even the breeze joins with a joyful hum,
As petals unite, twirling, they become one!

So bring out the snacks and the nectar so sweet,
In this flower fiesta, we can't be discreet.
For in every sway and twirl here at play,
Nature's frolic keeps the dullness at bay.

Secrets Hidden in Bloom

Underneath petals, there's mischief at play,
Secrets are whispered in a colorful way.
A violets' giggle shoots right through the air,
As tulips discuss who is wearing what flair.

Behind every leaf, there's a tale to tell,
Of bees with their crushes, and flowers that fell.
Lavender chuckles at the roses' stuck-up ways,
While marigolds plot for glory-filled days.

Ferns stretch their fronds in a sly little game,
"What's that? A bug? It could bring us some fame!"
Petals ponder if fortune will bloom,
As creatures tread lightly, avoiding the gloom.

So listen closely as the blossoms conspire,
Their secrets unravel, igniting the fire.
For in every fragrance, a jest holds its place,
In this garden of giggles, we all share the space.

Celestial Bloom's Embrace

In a garden where daisies dance,
The bees wear tuxedos, quite by chance.
Sunflowers gossip with giggles so loud,
While frogs in bow ties croak, oh so proud.

Petunias plot under the moon's sly grin,
Whispering secrets on a grassy din.
A daffodil jokes with a lazy bee,
"Why buzz around? Come dine with me!"

The daisies roll in a flower race,
While butterflies laugh, oh what a chase!
With pollen fights, they play all day,
Nature's own circus, in a floral ballet.

And when the night drapes its velvet cloak,
The blossoms snicker at every joke.
Their laughter lingers in the crisp air,
In a world where blooms flaunt without a care.

A Tangle of Vibrant Secrets

Roses hide secrets under their thorns,
While petunias boast of their colorful adorns.
A dandelion bloats when the breezes blow,
Saying, "Look at me, I'm the star of the show!"

Lilies laugh loudly, their fragrance in bloom,
Spreading wild rumors from their leafy room.
"Did you hear? That weed thinks he's a gem!"
They chuckle and snicker, a floral anthem.

Marigolds gossip in their golden hue,
"Can you believe the things that blooms do?"
With every bloom, there's a tale to share,
In this jolly garden, where joy fills the air.

And as the sun dips, they stifle a yawn,
These cheeky petals pull at the dawn.
Budding with mischief, their laughter spreads,
In a tangle of color, where whimsy threads.

Echoes in the Meadow

In a meadow bright, where daisies chime,
Ticklish winds laugh, keeping perfect time.
Each flower giggles, a playful broadcast,
Echoes of laughter, a moment to last.

Buttercups whisper, secrets in bloom,
While bees debate whether they'll grab a room.
The grass uproariously teases the breeze,
Swirling in circles, with maximum ease.

A daffodil tumbles, a fall so grand,
Becoming the star of this flower band.
The clover joins in, with a tiny cheer,
"Did you see that? I need a souvenir!"

When twilight falls over this frolicsome scene,
Stars twinkle above, oh, what a serene!
Nature's own jesters, in colors so bold,
In echoes of laughter, their tales unfold.

The Rainbow's Floral Canvas

A canvas of petals, in colors so bright,
Hibiscus winks in morning light.
The violets snicker at the sun's gold rays,
Sketching a portrait of whimsical days.

Crayons of blossoms paint the sky gray,
As geraniums giggle, come what may.
"Oh look, a tulip tripped on a bee!"
Laughter erupts, as fun as can be.

Lilacs swirl in a dancing spree,
Chasing the pollen like it's a decree.
Breezes join in, swirling perfectly tight,
Creating a tapestry that glimmers in light.

With each bloom a story, a splash of delight,
The garden rejoices, yearnings ignite.
In a rainbow's embrace, each flower plays,
A vibrant exhibition of joyful displays.

Dance of Blossoms in the Fields

In fields where daisies play,
The bumblebees buzz all day.
They wear tiny hats in style,
Twirl around with much ado and smile.

The violets giggle and sway,
With every breeze, they find their way.
While poppies toss their tiny heads,
Dancing madly, skipping threads.

A butterfly joins the fun,
In a tutu, it spins and runs.
Cheering blooms on every side,
Jumping jacks, they take in stride.

The sun sets low, they take a bow,
A floral show, oh wow, oh wow!
With petals bright, they end the spree,
In laughter's glow, wild and free.

An Ode to Flora's Grand Tapestry

A patchwork quilt of colors bright,
Each bloom vying for the light.
The lilies wear their shades of grace,
While dandelions prank in the race.

Roses brag of their sweet smell,
While marigolds cast a floral spell.
Sunflowers stand tall, full of cheer,
Boasting to bees that buzz so near.

In the meadow, a silly scene,
Tulips strut, feeling like queens.
With petals like skirts, they spin around,
In this crazy garden, laughter's found.

As twilight whispers to the space,
The flowers giggle, a happy chase.
An ode to blooms and their delight,
A funny fest that lasts all night.

Nature's Embroidery Underfoot

Dancing along the grassy route,
A rabbit hops in a little suit.
He trips on clover, giggles out loud,
And rolls like a button, oh so proud.

The daisies cheer, they don a cape,
Rooting for bumbles in their escape.
While stitch by stitch, the ground is set,
A crazy quilt of blooms, you bet!

Butterflies flit in hilarity,
Chasing shadows, what a rarity!
They sprinkle pollen, a vibrant dust,
With nature's humor, oh what a must!

In this tapestry of laughter's flow,
The earth beneath, a funny show.
A canvas bright, each petal sings,
Nature's mirth in all that springs.

Whispers of an Enchanted Meadow

In the meadow, whispers say,
That flowers have jokes for every day.
The lilacs giggle, sharing a pun,
While daisies tickle the lazy sun.

A sneaky squirrel plays a trick,
Jumping over blossoms, oh what a kick!
"Catch me if you can!" he shouts with glee,
As violets chuckle, "What will it be?"

The ferns shake their fronds in glee,
Making shadows, a playful spree.
With wild whimsies, they spin and turn,
In a dance of laughter, bright and fern.

As dusk falls softly, they rest for now,
With dreams of sunlight's playful vow.
A meadow filled with cheerful sighs,
Where laughter blooms beneath the skies.

Tangles of Earth and Sky

A dandelion danced in the breeze,
Socks on a rooster, oh, what a tease!
Butterflies giggled, a comical sight,
As ants played a game of hide and seek night.

Clouds wore mustaches, quite the bold sight,
A squirrel in shades, just caught the light.
Flowers threw parties under the sun,
While mushrooms got tipsy—oh, what fun!

The wind whispered secrets, a cheeky prank,
As petals raced each other in a lanky flank.
Nature's odd dancers twirled with glee,
In a garden where laughter is wild and free.

So here's to the quirks, the giggles, the grins,
Where nature holds parties, and everyone wins.
Through tangled knots of dirt and sky,
Mother Earth chuckles, a deep-rooted sigh.

Nature's Lullaby in Technicolor

In vibrant hues where the critters play,
A snail wore a hat, quite stylish, I say!
Grasshoppers croaked out a funky beat,
While daisies tapped toes in rhythmic heat.

A butterfly flutters, but where's it off to?
Oh wait, it's caught in a sticky goo!
Bees in tuxedos buzz with finesse,
Proposing to flowers in charming excess.

The sun beams down, causing shadows to prance,
While the frogs in the pond hold a wacky dance.
Nature's own band, a whimsical show,
With laughter and colors that steal the glow.

So let's skip 'round in this bright balmy bliss,
In technicolor dreams, how could we miss?
Each leaf laughs softly, and each flower hums,
In nature's funny tune, oh, how joy comes!

Fragments of a Floral Serenade

Petals in pirouettes, they twirl and spin,
A cactus complains—it's no fun to be thin!
Sunflowers wear shades, strutting with flair,
While tulips trade jokes with the breeze in the air.

The bees are the jesters, buzzing their lines,
Pollen party hats, they toast with good wines.
Buttercup giggles at the rose's tall tales,
While ferns try on wigs—shimmering veils.

A daisy asked, "Why do you bloom so bright?"
"Because," said the fern, "I'm just out of sight!"
In this floral realm where laughter does bloom,
Even the weeds have a penchant for zoom!

So gather your laughter, join the parade,
In fragments of echoes, sweet dreams are made.
Nature's serenade plays silly and bright,
Bringing joy to our hearts, a pure delight.

Harmonic Layers of Life

In the layers of greens and vibrant gold,
A flower snickered, "Hey, I'm not that old!"
A caterpillar crooned in a flowery mix,
While a grasshopper rapped to a funky fix.

Trees feigned a whisper, sharing old jokes,
While hedgehogs rolled by, smirking at blokes.
Life wrapped in laughter, a comical blend,
As nature awaits, ready to lend.

The rain fell in giggles, a ticklish embrace,
Each drop a dancer, in a wild chase.
Mountains chuckled, wearing snow like a hat,
While the valleys replied, "Well, imagine that!"

So let's stroll together, hand in hand,
In this harmonic life, where joy meets the land.
Each layer of laughter, a sweet serenade,
In a world full of wonders, mischief displayed.

Blossoms Against the Horizon

Bright daisies laugh in the breeze,
Tulips strut like they're at a tease.
Sunflowers swing their heavy heads,
While bees audition for floral threads.

Pansies whisper with cheeky grins,
Telling secrets of where the fun begins.
Dandelions dance in their own parade,
With wishes and giggles that never fade.

In the meadow, the bees' sweet hum,
Echoes of joy that make us all succumb.
Horizon dressed in colors so bold,
Laughter blooms as the stories unfold.

Each petal a giggle, a chuckle in bloom,
Nature's party, all filled with room.
As the sun dips low, the shadows eerily start,
Even the flowers play a part in the art.

Echoes of the Verdant Sea

In the green waves where grasses sway,
Squirrels debate who'll win today.
Dandelion fluff takes flight with a cheer,
While rabbits hop, erasing all fear.

The daisies chant, a quirky old rhyme,
Their roots intertwined in a dance with time.
A butterfly flutters, unsure of its way,
Like a confused kite on a windy day.

Violets gossip beneath the tall trees,
Tickled by whispers of the teasing breeze.
Playing hide and seek, they chuckle and pry,
While shy little ferns peek and sigh.

Each leaf a note in nature's grand song,
Echoing laughter where we all belong.
A sea of green, with giggles so free,
In this wild space, we just laugh with glee.

Petal-Paved Pathways

On a pathway paved with petals bright,
Bumblebees buzz with sheer delight.
Every step's a laugh, a hop, a skip,
As flowers offer their sweet little quips.

Marigolds boast of their sunny glow,
While lilies blush, hiding in the row.
With each little turn, the fun doesn't cease,
A treasure hunt for the tiniest piece.

The grass is a carpet, soft and lush,
Inviting all creatures to take a rush.
Curly-cue vines offer a silly show,
As they weave and twist, putting on a glow.

With petals as maps to this whimsical realm,
Nature's a ship with joy at the helm.
Every corner brimming with smiles so wide,
A joyful jaunt where fun can't hide.

Secrets of the Garden's Heart

In the garden's core, where laughter lies,
Chortles of critters and fluttering sighs.
A squirrel's caper, a chipmunk's cheer,
Make every moment a truthful veneer.

Roses twist their petals, gossip in bloom,
With secrets so sweet, they dispel all gloom.
Daffodils chuckle in bright golden tones,
While nightingales sing, abandoning their phones.

The soil still chuckles from stories of yore,
Of seeds that were planted right by the door.
With a wink from the daisies and nod from the thyme,
Every ounce of the garden wins with a rhyme.

As shadows grow longer, the fun stays alive,
In the heart of the garden, where chuckles thrive.
Where petals and laughter twirl in the air,
A playful reminder that joy's everywhere.

Flora's Embrace in the Breeze

Daisies dance like little clowns,
Tickling bees with silly frowns.
Buttercups wear their golden crowns,
Chasing squirrels in blooming gowns.

Tulips trumpet in a row,
Spilling secrets to the low.
'Hurry up!' the roses crow,
As petals drip with petals' flow.

In the gale, the petals swirl,
Like children lost in summer's whirl.
The daisies twist in frolic's twirl,
As butterflies give wings a whirl.

Glancing shoes from folks nearby,
Carefree laughs, oh my, oh my!
Nature bursts with colors high,
Marigolds shout, "Let's not be shy!"

Echoes of a Floral Memory

Remember when the blooms would sing,
A chorus loud of everything?
Forget-me-nots with tales to fling,
Accuse the frogs of crazy bling.

Dandelions, those bold pranksters,
Blow their fluff and cause disasters.
Ticklish winds play like masters,
While violets duel for laughter's blasters.

Roses whisper giggles sweet,
Lily pads slip, oh what a feat!
Nature's follies can't be beat,
In this kaleidoscope retreat.

Frogs wear ties, their chests all bare,
While dragonflies go-keek, beware!
In woodland jokes, we leave our care,
With floral laughter in the air.

The Language of Blooms

Lilies speak in scents and sighs,
While pansies plot their jokester cries.
Sunflowers wave, oh what a prize,
As laughter echoes through the skies.

Petunias scribble silly tales,
With every gust that flips their sails.
In this floral land, humor prevails,
As daisies race and twist their trails.

Marshmallow clouds of cotton candy,
Encourage blooms that sway so dandy.
With tiny gnomes who act quite handy,
Sprinkling jokes, oh so randy!

In a bouquet of giggles bright,
Colors clash in sheer delight.
The blooms unite in pure moonlight,
Flora's fun, oh what a sight!

In the Heart of the Meadow

In the meadow where the laughter grows,
Wildflowers bust their comical prose.
Bees bumping heads as friendship shows,
And through it all, a scent that glows.

Fields of daisies play hide and seek,
With grasses tickling every cheek.
Through every chat, they blurt and squeak,
The funniest place, oh so unique!

Butterflies with big ideas fly,
Painting jokes across the sky.
Poppies pout as time drifts by,
As crickets chirp a lullaby.

In this laughter-laden spree,
Nature's fun unveils with glee.
Here in blooms, we're wild and free,
In the heart where laughter's key!

A Canvas of Nature's Palette

Daisies dance with glee,
Buttercups join the spree.
The bees wear tiny hats,
While ants hold dance-off chats.

Fragrant breezes blow,
Tickling toes as they go.
Colors clash like paint,
Oh, who needs to be quaint?

Lemons and limes fight hard,
A citrus garden card.
While sunflowers cheer loud,
In a floral, funny crowd.

Nature's paintbrush spills,
Over valleys, thrills and chills.
Giggles echo in the breeze,
Oh, to be among the trees!

Beneath the Canopy of Green

Beneath the leafy dome,
Squirrels search for a home.
Chasing shadows, they leap,
As wise owls take a peep.

Frogs croak their own tunes,
Dancing under the moons.
While rabbits play hide and seek,
In a game quite unique.

The breeze teases the trees,
With laughter that's a tease.
Raccoons wear masks for style,
Yeah, they dance all the while!

Nature sings a song,
In this happy throng.
Beneath the laughing shade,
A jungle parade is made.

Colorful Stitches of the Earth

Petals pirouette bright,
As if in pure delight.
A patchwork quilt of cheer,
Bringing smiles far and near.

Jellybean grass so wide,
Where beetles love to ride.
A butterfly fashion show,
Oh, how they steal the show!

Crickets strum their guitar,
To moths that twirl like stars.
In a dance so ridiculous,
Life here is quite meticulous!

The earth's a nutty base,
With silly sounds and grace.
A vivid fabric we see,
Nature's quirky jubilee!

Hues of Harmony and Hope

Rainbows paint the sky,
While gophers dig nearby.
In a world filled with fun,
Where laughter's never done.

Blossoms tease the bees,
With sweet pollen to squeeze.
A parade of colors bright,
In a game of pure delight.

The daisies tell jokes,
While bright-eyed little folks.
Come together for a feast,
Nature's laughter - a beast!

In gardens where we play,
Life goes on in a sway.
A tapestry of cheer,
Funny moments, all year!

Beauty Unraveled by the Wind

A daisy danced, caught in a breeze,
It twirled so bold, with such great ease.
A squirrel laughed, shook his fluffy tail,
As petals swirled like a fairytale.

The roses whispered, "You think you're grand?"
While tulips sighed, "We're just as planned!"
With pollen hats, the bees took flight,
A floral party, oh what a sight!

Butterflies joined, in polka-dot suits,
The garden turned into kooky hoots.
A gust blew hard, oh what a mess,
Nature's comedy, we must confess.

So grab some seeds, and plant a giggle,
With every sprout, let laughter wiggle.
The flowers know the secret trace,
Of silly joy in this wild place.

The Enchantment of Springtime

The sun peeks out, a shy little star,
Buds laugh and shout, "Look how happy we are!"
The bunnies skip with their floppy ears,
Sprouting joy like wild, silly cheers.

Daffodils wearing hats made of dew,
Challenging each other, "Who looks the best, too?"
While tulips gossip across the bed,
"No way! That color is totally dead!"

Squirrels debate on the best nut treat,
While ants march by in their tiny fleet.
A breeze throws petals, a floral parade,
Nature's mischief, forever displayed.

This springtime magic, oh what a scene,
With laughter erupting, the garden's so keen.
Let's gather our giggles, come join the fest,
For all of creation knows how to jest!

Sun-kissed Blooms and Shadows

The sun drizzles honey on every petal,
While daisies hold music, they dance to the metal.
A dandelion yells, "I'm the king of the field!"
While sunflowers roll their eyes, they won't yield.

A butterfly winks, with a glittery grin,
"Catch me if you can, but can you begin?"
The wind plays tricks, like a jester so spry,
As tulips argue, "Wait, was that a pie?"

With shadows that stretch into giggly forms,
The garden erupts in whimsical storms.
An ant wears a crown made of leaf and glue,
Proclaiming, "All hail, the queen of the crew!"

In this bright patch where laughter blooms free,
Every flower knows it's the key to be glee.
So dance with the beetles, and chirp with delight,
For sun-kissed moments make everything right!

Nature's Artistry in the Open

A painter's palette spills on the grass,
With colors that shimmer as moments pass.
The daisies smirk at the bold marigolds,
"Bet you can't beat our dazzling folds!"

While violets chuckle, dressed in their best,
"Can you feel the heat? We're passing the test!"
The wind took a stroke, fresh and so wild,
As flowers giggled, each flower a child.

A caterpillar slips, tries to look grand,
"Watch out for me, I'm a rockstar, you'll see!"
But tripping along in the sun's warm glow,
Kept the garden alive with its charming show.

So let's grab our brushes, and splatter some cheer,
For nature's artistry sings loud and clear.
Embrace the fun in each petal's swirl,
In this colorful world where laughter unfurls!

Fables of the Blossom Trail

Once a bee with a penchant for dance,
Buzzed and twirled in a floral romance.
He slipped on a petal, fell flat on his face,
Shouting, "These daisies are not a safe place!"

A squirrel in shades tossed his acorn in style,
He thought it a ball for a sporty new trial.
But the acorn rolled off, straight into a brook,
"Well, that's a new sport—great job for a rook!"

With flowers discussing their latest trends,
A tulip declared, "I need better friends!"
A snapdragon said, "Well, let's have a feast,
Though I spill my tea, I'm just a flower beast!"

Thus the gossip of blossoms flowed loud and clear,
As petals exchanged tales with laughter to cheer.
Each bloom a comedian in nature's grand play,
Turning mundane moments to sideshow ballet.

Stitched with Nature's Hand

A hedgehog in bowtie, so finely dressed,
Said, "I can't find my flowers—I've been overly stressed!"

He snoozed on a daisy, then came to a flair,
"I'll accessorize with this lovely brown hair!"

Bunnies in bonnets pranced all around,
Chasing their tails without making a sound.
"I think I saw carrots but now they're all gone,"
"They're having a party, let's see who's won!"

With petals for napkins, and daisies for drinks,
The frogs sang their songs while the garden winks.
"Is this a garden or a carnival spree?"
"We'll just call it spring, can't you see?"

A butterfly giggled at a snail with a hat,
Said, "You wear it well; doesn't matter you're flat!"
So whenever they gathered, the fun never ceased,
In the land of the greenery, they thrived as a feast.

Chronicles of the Blossom Grove

In a grove where the colors danced with delight,
A caterpillar boasted, "I'm the fastest in flight!"
But just as he claimed, and took off real fast,
He tripped on a twig—his glory didn't last.

A wise old owl perched in a lilac so grand,
Weaving tales of the fun on his big fuzzy stand.
"Every bloom has a secret, even us here!
Like the rose that swears it makes the best beer!"

Two daisies doing a jig in the grass,
Twirled around until one lost her sass.
"Step on my petals again, and I swear,
I'll summon my friends from the butterfly lair!"

With laughter that echoed through branches and leaves,
Each critter rejoiced, basked in the eves.
"Let's throw a shindig!" a bumblebee shouted,
And soon all the blooms were utterly glouted!

Nature's Bioluminescent Palettes

In the twilight, where colors glow bright,
A glow-worm grinned, aiming for flight.
"Catch me if you can!" shouted fern to the vine,
But the fern would stumble—'twas not its design!

The flowers were buzzing with stories of glee,
While tadpoles rehearsed their ballet by the sea.
"Watch me pirouette!" announced the proud frog,
As he slipped on a lily—what a comedic slog!

An evening with crickets brought chuckles and cheer,
"Why did the leaf take up opera this year?"
A fun-loving moth, in a saner embrace,
Winked at the moon while the stars kept the pace.

Nature's own palette, with laughter all night,
In the wild glowing hues, everything felt right.
For nothing compares to this kind of delight,
Where every small creature is ready to bite!

Petals and the Poetry of Seasons

In springtime's embrace, the daisies debate,
Who's fluffiest here? They cannot wait.
The tulips giggle, their colors so bold,
As bumblebees dance, their antics unfold.

Summer sun laughs as butterflies flit,
"Is that your best pose? Come on, admit!"
Petals all puffed, in a bright, breezy swirl,
Even the thorns have found ways to twirl.

As autumn arrives, leaves take a bow,
"Old man winter, don't rush us now!"
They whirl and they twirl in coppery hues,
While squirrels play tag, dodging all the blues.

With winter's soft cloak, snowflakes will twirl,
"Think we can dance? Oh, give it a whirl!"
The garden now snoozes, wrapped up tight,
But dreams of the blooms are a comical sight.

Dappled Sunlight on Floral Dreams

Under the oaks, in the dappled light,
Petunias gossip, sharing delight.
"Did you see that bee, so clumsy and round?
He bumped into me and fell to the ground!"

Sunflowers beam, with their faces so big,
"Here comes a bug dancing a jiggly jig!"
They sway with the breeze, making quite the show,
In a garden carnival, laughter will flow.

The violets whisper, "We're shy, it's true,
But did you hear what the roses can do?"
A joke about thorns leaves everyone chuckling,
Rainbow-hued petals are endlessly snickering.

Beneath all the blooms, the worms play pranks,
Digging tiny tunnels, giving garden thanks.
The flowers all giggle, with roots deep in play,
While dappled sunlight continues to sway.

Sing the Song of Colors

Oh, sing me the song of the vibrant blooms,
Where violets dance and the daisies zoom.
"Hey, what's that noise?" chirp the zinnias bright,
"It's just the sun singing, a sweet delight!"

The roses pipe up, "We're the fairest of all!"
But the daisies just chuckle, "Who made that call?"
In a garden that giggles, no petal feels shy,
As colors unite under the wide, open sky.

With every bright hue, the humor just grows,
Carnivals happen, wherever it flows.
Carnation jokes circling, "I'm the best!"
But solidarity reigns, no time for a jest.

So if you feel down, come visit our land,
Where petals are friends and help you to stand.
In the garden's embrace, let your worries melt,
With a song of pure colors, laughter is felt.

Along the Trails of Petal-Laden Dreams

On trails where flowers carpet the ground,
A butterfly slips, saying, "Look what I found!"
The daisies all giggle, whispering sweet,
"Watch your step there, and aim for the beat!"

With every bright turn, a funny story flows,
"Did you hear the one about the flowering bows?"
They swap all the tales, petals swaying with cheer,
Each punchline blooms brightly, bringing delight near.

As poppies join in, bursting red and bold,
They share their own twist on a nursery told.
In this realm of blossoms, giggles are grand,
From morning to night, hand in hand they stand.

So come walk the paths, feel the joy in the breeze,
Where laughter's the nectar among vibrant trees.
In the land of the petal-laden dreams we find,
A tapestry woven from humor combined.

Lullabies from the Colorful Expanse

In the fields where daisies sway,
Bumblebees join in a clumsy ballet.
The sunflowers nod, what a sight to see,
They're gossiping softly, as proud as can be.

A ladybug rolls on the grass in a spin,
Chasing its dreams with a goofy grin.
Grasshoppers giggle, they hop right along,
Singing their tunes, always coming on strong.

The violets blush at the jokes from the rye,
"Did you hear about daisies? They just can't fly!"
The wind joins in with a chuckle and swish,
While butterflies dance like they're making a wish.

In this patch of humor, the world feels just right,
Where the petals are playful, and the bugs take to flight.
So if you are weary, come join the fun,
In the laughs of the flowers, beneath the warm sun.

Banner of the Untamed Meadow

In a meadow where tigers ride on a breeze,
A snail with a top hat gets stuck in a tease.
The clovers all giggle, the daisies are wild,
As the dandelions pout, "We were here first, child!"

A butterfly calls out, "Let's start a parade!"
They march round the daisies; they're never afraid.
The rowdy old thistles push back with a grin,
"Who knew that our garden could cause such a din?"

With petals that flutter like banners of cheer,
They plot a grand scheme to take over the sphere.
But when the sun sets, they all take a nap,
In the banner of chaos, they form a sweet trap.

So if you wander, just stop and you'll see,
The tales of this meadow invite you for tea.
With laughter and tales from the petals so bright,
Where the universe chuckles at day and at night.

The Palette of Wild Existence

Brushes of color splash across the ground,
With paint-stained bees buzzing all around.
A poppy says, "Red is the color of fun!"
While tulips in purple say, "We're better than sun!"

The artist of nature has chosen this scene,
Where petals of laughter and mischief convene.
The buttercups play tug-of-war with the breeze,
While sage shouts, "More spice! Let's tickle the trees!"

"Who shrunk the daisies?" a willow tree sighs,
As rabbits frolic, conspiring with flies.
The colors are swirling, a festival rare,
And each bloom is laughing, without a care.

In this palette of jesters, the world's quite absurd,
Every flower a storyteller, each bug is a bird.
So step right on in, for the giggles are free,
In the canvas of chaos, where we all want to be.

Fantasies of the Flowering World

The whimsical daisies scheme in the sun,
"Let's throw a party! It'll be so much fun!"
They'll dance on the breeze, with a twist and a hop,
While the orchids and lilies can't help but stop.

A bee in a tuxedo is ready to sing,
With flowers as dancers, it's quite the spring fling!
The ants form a line; they're cleaning up crumbs,
Cheering each other, "Let us enjoy the drums!"

The petals are strumming with joy in the air,
A melody rising, where few have a care.
The violets spin, caught up in a dream,
While the roses look on and squint at the gleam.

In this flowering world, humor reigns bold,
As nature spins stories, eternally told.
So join in the laughter, don't wait, come and play,
For the magic of flowers will brighten your day!

Petals in the Breeze

Bees buzzing loudly, what a funny sight,
Dancing 'round flowers, from morning to night.
They tickle the petals, oh what a thrill,
While the daisies giggle, standing quite still.

One dandy lion boasts a golden mane,
Claims he's the king of the flower lane.
But tulips just shrug with a playful cheer,
"In all this pollen, you're still just a deer!"

A bumblebee sneezes, oh what a mess,
Spills all his nectar, what could be less?
Lilies laugh loudly, it's quite the parade,
As butterflies flutter, their joy won't fade.

So gather your laughter, let worries take flight,
In gardens of giggles, everything's bright.
The blooms sing together in colors so grand,
A symphony vibrant, by nature's own hand.

Threads of Nature's Quilt

Threads of sunshine, bright and bold,
Stitch all the stories that nature has told.
A spider with glasses counts every stitch,
While soft moss giggles, feeling quite rich.

A busy old worm takes weaving requests,
While robins debate who can make the best nests.
But grasshoppers say, with a mischievous grin,
"It's definitely us; we've got the best spin!"

A dandelion's fluff takes a ride in the wind,
While violets laugh, "What a wild little friend!"
They twirl 'round in circles, all merry and bright,
Underneath the warm glow of the moonlight.

So grab your big needles, let's knit up some cheer,
With petals and laughter, we'll craft all the year.
Each stitch is a giggle, a smile to unveil,
In this quilt of delight, we'll merrily sail.

Tapestry of Earthly Blooms

A quirky collection of quirky blooms,
Bursting with laughter, dispersing the glooms.
The violets boast of their royal blue hue,
While dandelions declare, "We're best—that's true!"

The poppies march on with their ruffled red flair,
Saying, "We're famous! We don't have a care!"
But tulips just snicker, their heads held up high,
"Your fame is but folly, as the bees buzz by!"

The sunflowers gossip, they're six feet tall,
"Who's the silliest bloom? Well, that's not our call!"
The daisies implore, with a "Hearts all aglow,"
"Let's spread this joy, come on, let's go!"

So come, grab a petal, and wear it with pride,
In this tapestry bright, let your laughter abide.
We'll twirl and we'll giggle on this whimsical ride,
With colors and humor, oh what a side!

Meadow's Whispering Colors

In meadows where hues seem to giggle and dance,
The violets whisper, hey, come take a chance!
The sun shines down, spreading smiles all around,
While butterflies trade all their secrets, unbound.

Bees wear their tuxedos, quite stylish indeed,
While ladybugs prance, they will surely succeed.
A cloud overhead drizzles sparkles of cheer,
As daisies declare, "It's the best time of year!"

The mushrooms all hide, in their polka dot suits,
And giggle at leaves, in their rustling flutes.
A rabbit pops up with a carrot in hand,
"Why not join the dance? It's simply grand!"

So come to this meadow, let laughter abound,
In a rainbow of colors where joy can be found.
Share whispers of fun, let your spirit take flight,
For the world is a canvas that's painted just right.

The Artistry of Untamed Fields

Bees in disco, flying high,
All the petals wave goodbye.
Sunflowers wear their sunny hats,
While daisies gossip like chattering cats.

Buttercups throw a bold parade,
With butterflies in a grand charade.
Grasshoppers chirp their comic tune,
While ladybugs dance under the moon.

Lavender laughs, dressed in hue,
While orchids tease in morning dew.
Fields of color, a playful sight,
Nature's canvas, pure delight.

So if you stroll past the daisies' cheer,
Prepare for laughter; the flowers are near!
With every step, a comedic vibe,
In untamed fields, joy will prescribe.

Floral Stories in the Wind

Petunias gossip, sharing tales,
Of butterflies with funny trails.
Lilies chuckle, swaying light,
In a world of pollen, taking flight.

The wind carries whispers, oh so sly,
As tulips gossip and the clouds comply.
A dandelion sneezes, seeds in a spree,
Sprinkling wishes, wild and free.

Irises giggle, dressed so bold,
Telling stories of days of old.
Carnations conspire, what fun indeed,
In the floral air, laughter's the seed.

If you listen close, you might just find,
That flowers have stories, and they're quite unaligned!
Their petals play tricks, in the soft daylight,
In the tales of blooms, everything feels bright.

Dance of the Wilds

Dandelions do the cha-cha, it's true,
While clovers twist, in a bright green hue.
Bluebells jive, swaying in the breeze,
With tiny ants busting moves with ease.

Sunflowers spin, their heads held high,
While the daisies leap, oh my! oh my!
Hummingbirds zip, in a flittering ball,
A joyous dance, inviting us all.

Every butterfly joins the fest,
In this floral party, they're truly blessed.
Grass is the floor, underfoot it feels,
In the dance of the wilds, no one heels.

So bring your giggles, your best dance shoes,
The flowers are waiting, letting joy ooze.
With every twirl in this lively land,
You'll find happiness, oh so grand!

A Symphony of Fragrant Hues

Roses blush, playing the flute,
While violets harmonize, oh what a hoot!
A concert of scents in the sunlit air,
With every bloom joining in their flair.

Chrysanthemums beat the drum so loud,
While poppies sway, feeling proud.
Peonies sing their sweet refrain,
In this fragrant symphony, laughter remains.

The tulips clap in a splash of cheer,
Making music that draws us near.
In fields of color, a joyful tune,
With every note, we dance till noon.

So breathe it in, this joyous sound,
In nature's orchestra, laughter's found.
Every flower tells a joke or two,
In this symphony of hues, bright and true.

A Journey Through Fields of Wonder

Bouncing bumblebees hum along,
They dance and dip in the warm sun's glow.
Grass tickles toes, and what a song!
Is that a sheep or a rapping crow?

Dandelions laugh, so bold and bright,
They sneak into hair like silly clowns.
Ants march in lines, a comical sight,
Sampling crumbs from our picnic towns.

A butterfly flaps with flair and ease,
Then trips on a petal, oh what a tease!
Nature's chaos brings laughs like breeze,
Who'd blame the flowers for their mischief, please?

So grab your snacks and join the cheer,
In fields of wonder, there's fun to share.
Nature's giggles are always near,
With sticky jam on your toes? Beware!

The Allure of Nature's Bounty

Nature's buffet is open wide,
With berries that bubble and cherries that sing.
We snack on petals, quite satisfied,
Though that bee thinks it owns everything!

Mushrooms, oh mushrooms, a quirky delight,
Some look like umbrellas—could they hold rain?
But who needs a drink when the sun shines bright?
Just watch your step; they can cause you pain!

A squirrel steals peaches, what a bold thief,
Trading his nuts for our juicy prize.
One glance at his face, full of mischief and grief,
You can't help but giggle at his surprise!

So tread with care in this sparkling feast,
With nature as chef, there's laughter galore.
The cracks in the path are where joy has increased,
And every little critter keeps us asking for more!

Mosaics of Color and Fragrance

Laughter erupts in nature's grand show,
Where petals parade like a colorful crew.
Poppies in red, and daisies in tow,
Who knew that flowers could dance like a shrew?

The lavender lays down a fragrant track,
While tulips flex their petals with flair.
And look at that daffodil in yellow slack,
It seems to trip over its own haughty air!

Butterflies play games in the blue-sky tide,
With each flutter a joke, they twist and swirl.
Is that one trying to hitch a ride?
Oh, hold on tight; it's a flower whirl!

In this garden where chuckles abound,
Every bloom's a partner in a fun, wild laugh.
Rolling in petals, we tumble around,
Nature's own comedy—take a photograph!

A Celebration of Verdant Life

Green leaves wave like they're at a show,
Roots tickle the ground with a sneaky tease.
Insects take charge, steal the whole flow,
They're the lively dancers, if you please!

Trees hold a summit, their branches all sway,
Debating the best shade spot for a nap.
While squirrels protest against the fray,
Chasing their tails in a comedic slap!

Giggling ferns whisper secrets off-stage,
As the sun slips in, causing mischief at noon.
Grasshoppers leap like they're breaking the cage,
And sing to the chorus of flowers in tune.

So raise a toast to the greenery bright,
In this wild adventure, we find our place.
With laughter echoing from morning till night,
Join the verdant life and embrace every space!

www.ingramcontent.com/pod-product-compliance
Lightning Source LLC
Chambersburg PA
CBHW071854160426
43209CB00003B/550